Anaconda

by Grace Hansen

SOUTH AMERICAN ANIMALS

Abdo Kids Jumbo is an Imprint of Abdo Kids
abdobooks.com

abdobooks.com

Published by Abdo Kids, a division of ABDO, P.O. Box 398166, Minneapolis, Minnesota 55439.
Copyright © 2023 by Abdo Consulting Group, Inc. International copyrights reserved in all countries.
No part of this book may be reproduced in any form without written permission from the publisher.
Abdo Kids Jumbo™ is a trademark and logo of Abdo Kids.

Printed in the United States of America, North Mankato, Minnesota.

052022

092022

 THIS BOOK CONTAINS
RECYCLED MATERIALS

Photo Credits: Alamy, Getty Images, Minden Pictures, Science Source, Shutterstock

Production Contributors: Teddy Borth, Jennie Forsberg, Grace Hansen
Design Contributors: Candice Keimig, Victoria Bates

Library of Congress Control Number: 2021950569
Publisher's Cataloging-in-Publication Data

Names: Hansen, Grace, author.

Title: Anaconda / by Grace Hansen.

Description: Minneapolis, Minnesota : Abdo Kids, 2023 | Series: South American animals | Includes online
    resources and index.

Identifiers: ISBN 9781098261818 (lib. bdg.) | ISBN 9781098262655 (ebook) | ISBN 9781098263072
    (Read-to-Me ebook)

Subjects: LCSH: Anaconda--Juvenile literature. | Snakes--Juvenile literature. | South America--Juvenile
    literature. | Rain forest animals--Juvenile literature. | Zoology--Juvenile literature.

Classification: DDC 597.96--dc23

Table of Contents

South America

South America is filled with lovely landscapes, from rain forests to mountain ranges. Because of these special places, a **diverse** group of animals live on the **continent**. Anacondas are just some of these animals.

North
America

Europe

Asia

Africa

South
America

5

Anacondas

Anacondas live in South America's **tropical** areas, especially the Amazon rainforest. Their favorite habitats are near swamps, marshes, and streams.

yellow anaconda

Amazon rainforest

There are four species of anacondas. The green anaconda is the largest. It is one of the world's heaviest and longest snakes.

green anaconda

An anaconda's colors depend on the species. But the snakes are often darker in color and spotted with green, brown, or yellow. This helps them blend in with their surroundings.

Green anacondas can grow to be 30 feet (9 m) long! They can weigh more than 500 pounds (227 kg). Other species are usually less than 15 feet (4.6 m) long and less than 100 pounds (45.5 kg).

Because of their size, it can be hard for anacondas to move on land. So, they are often found in water. The giant snakes can move easily there!

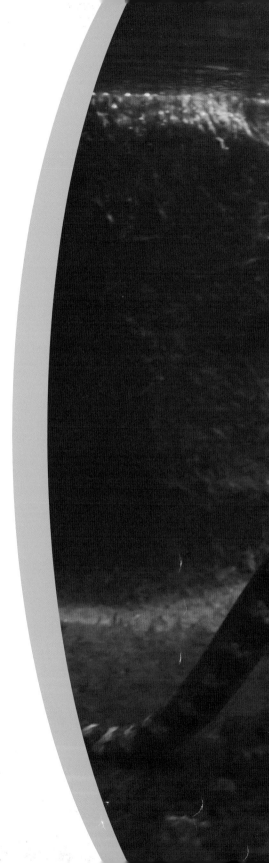

Hunting

Anacondas mainly hunt at night. They do not have **venom** to kill **prey**. Instead, they squeeze their prey. Then they swallow it whole!

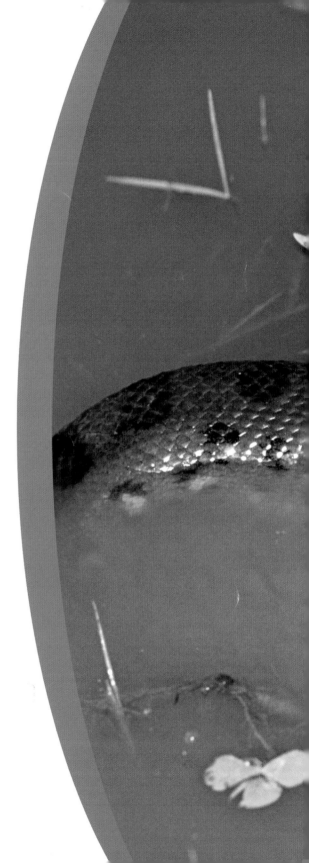

17

Baby Anacondas

Males and females come together to have young in April or May. After six months, baby snakes hatch inside their mother. Then the mother gives birth to 20 to 40 live young.

Baby anacondas are up to

2 feet (0.6 m) long at birth.

They are ready to live and

hunt on their own right away.

21

More Facts

- Anacondas are a large group of snakes of the genus *Eunectes*. *Eunectes* comes from a Greek word that means "good swimmer."

- Anacondas eat prey of all sizes. Big meals can keep them full for weeks!

- These snakes live for about 10 to 12 years in the wild. In captivity, they can live for 30 years. And they never stop growing!

Glossary

continent – one of the earth's seven major areas of land. The continents are Africa, Antarctica, Asia, Australia, Europe, North America, and South America.

diverse – of different kinds or sorts.

genus – a large group of different but closely related animals. It contains more organisms than a species.

prey – an animal that is hunted by other animals for food.

species – a group of living things that look alike and can have young together.

tropical – having a climate in which there is no frost and where plants can grow all year long.

venom – the poison that certain snakes and other animals produce.

Index